REAL POWER
FOR KIDS

KNOWING THE HOLY SPIRIT
AS YOUR FRIEND

by Rod Baker

Harrison House

Illustrations by Stephen Gilpin

21 20 19 18   18 17 16 15

Real Power for Kids:
Knowing the Holy Spirit as Your Friend
ISBN 13: 978-1-57794-707-3
ISBN 10: 1-57794-707-X
Copyright © 2005 by Roderick D. Baker
P.O. Box 701286
Tulsa, OK 74170

Published by Harrison House, Inc.

Dedication

To Amber—my winner!

Acknowledgments

Thank you to my wife, Gloria, who is the glory of my life. Also, special thanks to Pastors Billy Joe and Sharon Daugherty, to Victory Christian Center, and to the Victory Kidz Ministry staff—thank you for your support and compassion for reaching boys and girls.

Getting Started

The Holy Spirit is a gift from God to you—and everyone who accepts Jesus as his or her Savior. He will be your helper to guide you and help you know how to pray. He will comfort you when you feel afraid or alone.

Read along, and we will walk you through every step you need to take to receive the power of the Holy Spirit.

A Promise From God

The gift of the Holy Spirit has been promised by God for a long time. John the Baptist preached about it. Jesus told His disciples about the Holy Spirit. Before Jesus returned to heaven after His work on earth, He told them to wait in the city of Jerusalem until they received power from heaven.

That is exactly what they did. On the day of Pentecost, one hundred and twenty men were all praying. They were praying the same thing. They were praying for the promise of the Holy Spirit.

The Holy Spirit Comes

Suddenly, there was a sound like a mighty rushing wind. Something that looked like fire appeared in the room and landed on each person. When that happened, they were all filled with the Holy Spirit and began to speak with an unknown language as the Spirit gave them the words to say.

The Holy Spirit filled all the people in the room. No one was left behind. Everyone received the promise. The Holy Spirit works the same way today. Everyone can receive.

The disciples left the Upper Room in power. From that moment on, they were changed. They spoke in the temple. They preached from prisons. They healed the sick and the lame. It was like Jesus was there again doing the miracles, but this time, God was using His Holy Spirit-filled disciples.

You can receive the power of the Holy Spirit. You can have the same power that they had in the Bible. God has made sure that every person has been given the gift. It's yours for the taking. All you need to do is accept Jesus as your Savior and receive the gift by faith.

Speaking in Tongues

The day of Pentecost was the first time ever that the Holy Spirit filled believers to speak with other tongues. After that, there were many more times groups of people received the power of the Holy Spirit. Each time they did, speaking in an unknown language, or tongues, was present. It was the evidence, or proof, that people had received the power of the Holy Spirit. You will speak in other tongues, too, when you receive the power of the Holy Spirit.

It Is a Free Gift

Anything that God has for you is free. *Free!* Absolutely free. You couldn't pay for it if you wanted to. That is because Jesus already paid the price for every gift you need. Salvation is free! Healing is free! The gift of the Holy Spirit is free, too!

You cannot earn it or pay for it. It's free! All you need to do is accept it.

It's like this. On your birthday your parent gives you a present. You don't have to work for your present. You don't have to beg for your present. You just receive it because it was bought for you.

Receiving the power of the Holy Spirit is the same way. God is handing you a gift. You don't beg or talk God into it. You just reach out and receive it. And it's that easy because it belongs to you.

How To Receive the Power of the Holy Spirit

You don't need to pray for a long time asking God to give you the power of the Holy Spirit. Remember, the gift is already yours. You are just receiving what is yours to begin with.

The Holy Spirit has a part to do *and* you have a part to do. As the Holy Spirit fills you, He gives you the words to say. It's the Holy Spirit's job to give you the language or words to say.

Your part is to open your mouth and speak those words or sounds or languages. You may make one sound or maybe many different sounds. This is what we call "other tongues" or an "unknown language." You resist the desire to talk in English and yield or give way to the words the Spirit is giving you. It's not something in your mind, but something that comes from down in your spirit man.

You can pray to receive the Holy Spirit anywhere. In fact, believe you receive when you pray and it will be done for you. Remember your part: you do the talking. The Spirit does the filling. When you begin to speak your new language, it may seem strange at first, but stick with it.

Here is a prayer to help you:

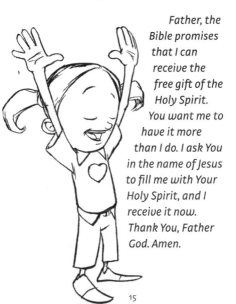

Father, the Bible promises that I can receive the free gift of the Holy Spirit. You want me to have it more than I do. I ask You in the name of Jesus to fill me with Your Holy Spirit, and I receive it now. Thank You, Father God. Amen.

Every Day With the Holy Spirit

Now that you have received this wonderful gift from God, you need to make it a part of your everyday life. You can pray at any time or any place you want to. You can pray in tongues beside your bed, on your way to school, playing in the park, standing on your head, or even in the shower. Wherever and whenever you want to, you can do it.

Don't be concerned that you only speak a few words in other tongues. As you pray more, more words appear in your language. It takes some time. Be patient.

You won't understand these words either. That's okay. The Bible says that when we pray in other tongues, we speak mysteries in the spirit. Our minds are not aware and don't understand the meaning of what our spirits are praying to God. Yet the Bible says that your prayers in other tongues are prayed perfectly and delivered to God.

The devil will try to steal the Word of God from your heart. He will try to tell you that you didn't really receive the power of the Holy Spirit. He will tell you that you are just making this up yourself. But remember, he is the father of lies. And if that is the case, then he must be lying to you as well. Just go back to God's Word and remember that God promised this gift to you.

What Praying in Tongues Does

Helps us remember that
God is always with us.

Speaking in tongues is a great
way to stay aware of God in our
everyday life. We feel comfortable
and secure knowing He is with us
all the time. (Heb. 13:6.)

Allows the Holy Spirit to help us.

The Holy Spirit is our helper. He has been called alongside us to help. The Holy Spirit is not doing the praying; we are. Yet He is helping us. That means more of our prayers are being answered. (John 14:16 NAS.)

Helps us know what to pray about.

There are times that we cannot think of how to pray. Our minds cannot think the problem out. Yet, thank God, the Holy Spirit knows all truth and leads our spirit in the exact prayer that is right for the situation. (Rom. 8:26.)

Helps us pray according to God's will.

Sometimes on their own people don't pray God's will. They don't do it on purpose, they just don't know the right way to pray. But the Holy Spirit searches the mind of God, prays according to His will, and leads you in a prayer that always works. (Rom. 8:27.)

MIND OF GOD

Helps us increase our faith.

The Bible tells us that we build up ourselves on our most holy faith, praying in the Spirit. It's like the Holy Spirit supercharges our faith when we pray in tongues. It would be like trying to saw a limb of a tree with a saw. It might take you until dinner time to get done sawing. But if you break out the chainsaw, you will be done before you break a sweat. (Jude 1:20.)

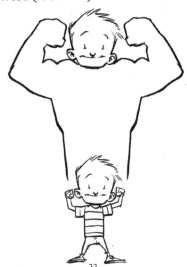

Builds your spirit up.

As a kid I used to love playing with battery operated toys until the batteries began to get low. The toys would slow down and lose their power. We are like that, too. When we spend a lot of time giving to the work of God, our spirits get weaker like a battery does in a toy. Praying in tongues helps us to recharge our batteries. Praying in other tongues builds us up in every area of our lives. (Jude 1:20.)

Helps you pray about the future.

One of the jobs of the Holy Spirit is to show us "things to come." When we pray in tongues we can get a sneak preview of what God is about to do. Now, you won't know who won the Super Bowl in advance, but you can understand what's coming ahead for your life. (Jer. 29:11.)

GOD'S FUTURE PLANS FOR YOU

Finishing Strong

History is full of examples of what men and women full of the Holy Spirit have been able to accomplish for God. You can accomplish great things, too! Pray often in the Spirit, and you will see your life in Christ grow beyond your wildest dreams. It's up to you. When you pray in tongues, the impossible becomes possible.

Share this precious gift with your friends. This gift is for everyone from the new believer to those who have been Christians for a long time. This gift is for the Charismatic churches, the Methodists, the Catholics, the Baptists, the Presbyterians, and the list goes on and on. If someone knows Jesus as his or her Savior, the person should know the Holy Spirit as a helper as well as a power source to help the person do what God wants him or her to do.

Prayer of Salvation

Father, I believe that Jesus died on the cross for my sins. I believe that He rose from the dead so that I can live with Him forever. I ask You to forgive me of my sins. I ask You to come into my heart and be the Lord (boss) of my life. I confess with my mouth that I am born again. Thank You for saving me. Amen.

About the Author

PASTOR ROD BAKER has served for over 20 years in children's and outreach ministry. He currently serves as director of the children ministries at Victory Christian Center in Tulsa, Oklahoma. He ministers to more than 4,000 children each week through children's church, bus ministry, Sidewalk Sunday School Trucks, and Kidz Clubs, as well as a food pantry which feeds over 2,000 people a month.

Under Rod's direction, the Victory Kidz School of Ministry is training up children's and youth workers for this millennium, while his newly developed "Leaders in Training" program is producing the same from our inner city youth. Rod has successfully taken hundreds of children on mission trips, integrating the curriculum being taught in all the children's ministries.

Rod and his wife, Gloria, reside in Tulsa with their children.

To contact Rod Baker
please write to:

P.O. Box 701286
Tulsa, OK 74170

Other Books by Rod Baker

Real Life for Kids
Knowing Jesus as Your Savior

Real Healing for Kids
Knowing Jesus as Your Healer

Fast. Easy.
Convenient.

For the latest Harrison House product
information and author news, look no
further than your computer. All the details
on our powerful, life-changing products are
just a click away. New releases, E-mail
subscriptions, Podcasts, testimonies,
monthly specials—find it all in one place.
Visit harrisonhouse.com today!

harrisonhouse

The Harrison House Vision

Proclaiming the truth and the power
Of the Gospel of Jesus Christ
With excellence;

Challenging Christians to
Live victoriously,
Grow spiritually,
Know God intimately.